ID0571582

The Kingship of Self-Control

The Kingship
of
Self-Control

William George Jordan

FLEMING H. REVELL COMPANY
OLD TAPPAN, NEW JERSEY

Printed in the United States of America

Contents

I. The Kingship of Self-Control   7

II. The Crimes of the Tongue   14

III. The Red Tape of Duty   20

IV. The Supreme Charity of the World   26

V. Worry, the Great American Disease   32

VI. The Greatness of Simplicity   38

VII. Living Life over Again   45

VIII. Syndicating Our Sorrows   51

IX. The Revelations of Reserve Power   58

CONTENTS

I. The Freedom of Self-Control
II. The Course of the Temple
III. The Right and Duty
IV. The Eternal Expression
V. ... the Concept of the Divine
VII. ... and Human Nature
VIII. Supreme Dominion
IX. The Justification of Knowledge?

I

The Kingship of Self-Control

Man has two creators—his God and himself. His first creator furnishes him the raw material of his life and the laws in conformity with which he can make that life what he will. His second creator—himself—has marvelous powers he rarely realizes. It is what a man makes of himself that counts.

When a man fails in life he usually says, "I am as God made me." When he succeeds he proudly proclaims himself a "self-made man." Man is placed in this world not as a finality but as a possibility. Man's greatest enemy is himself. Man in his weakness is the creature of circumstances; man in his strength is the creator of circumstances. Whether he be victim or victor depends largely on himself.

Man is never truly great merely for what he *is,* but ever for what he may become. Until man is truly filled with the knowledge of the majesty of his possibility, until there comes to him the glow of realization of his privilege to live the life committed to him as an individual life for which he is individually responsible, he is merely groping through the years.

To see his life as he might make it, man must go up alone into the mountains of spiritual thought as Christ went alone into the Garden, leaving the world to get strength to live in the world. He must there breathe the fresh, pure air of recognition of his divine importance as an indivdual, and with mind purified and tingling with new strength he must approach the problems of his daily living.

Man needs less of the "I am a feeble worm of the dust" idea in his theology, and more of the conception of "I am a great human soul with marvelous possibilities" as a vital element in his daily, working religion. With this broadening, stimulating view of life, he sees how he may attain his kingship through self-control. And the self-control that is seen in the most spectacular instances in history, and in the simplest phases of daily life is precisely the same in kind and in quality, differing only in degree. This control man can attain, if he only will; it is but a matter of paying the price.

The power of self-control is one of the great qualities that differentiates man from the lower animals. He is the only animal capable of a moral struggle or a moral conquest.

Every step in the progress of the world has been a new "control." It has been escaping from the tyranny of a fact to the understanding and mastery of that fact. For ages man looked in terror at the lightning flash; today he has begun to understand it as electricity, a force he has mastered and made his slave. The million phases of electrical invention are but manifestations of our control over a great force. But the greatest of all "control" is self-control.

At each moment of man's life he is either a king or a slave. As he surrenders to a wrong appetite, to any human weakness, as he falls prostrate in hopeless subjection to any condition, to any environment, to any failure, he is a slave. As he day by day crushes out human weakness, masters opposing elements within him, and day by day re-creates a new self from the sin and folly of his past—then he is a king. He is a king ruling with wisdom over himself. Alexander conquered the whole world—except Alexander. Emperor of the earth, he was the servile slave of his own passions.

We look with envy upon the possessions of others and wish they were our own. Sometimes we feel this in a vague, dreamy way with no thought of real attainment. Sometimes, however, we grow bitter, storm at the wrong distribution of the good things of life, and then relapse into a hopeless fatalistic acceptance of our condition.

We envy the success of others, when we should emulate the process by which that success came.

We may sometimes envy the power and spiritual strength of a Paul, without realizing the weak Saul of Tarsus from which he was transformed through his self-control.

We shut our eyes to the thousands of instances of the world's successes—mental, moral, physical, financial or spiritual—wherein the great final success came from a beginning far weaker and poorer than our own.

Any man may attain self-control if he only will. He must not expect to gain it save by long-continued payment of price, in small progressive expenditures of energy. Nature is a thorough believer in the installment plan in her relations with the individual. No man is so poor that he cannot *begin* to pay for what he wants; and every small, individual payment that he makes, Nature stores and accumulates for him as a reserve fund in his hour of need.

The patience man expends in bearing the little trials of his daily life Nature stores for him as a wondrous reserve in a crisis of life. With Nature, the mental, the physical or the moral energy he expends daily in right-doing is all stored for him and transmuted into strength. Nature never accepts a cash payment in full for anything—this would be an injustice to the poor and to the weak.

It is only the progressive installment plan Nature recognizes. No man can make a habit in a moment or break it in a moment. It is a matter of development, of growth. But at any moment man may *begin* to make or begin to break any habit. This view of the growth of character should be a mighty stimulus to the man who sincerely desires and determines to live nearer to the limit of his possibilities.

Self-control may be developed in precisely the same manner as we tone up a weak muscle, by little exercises day by day. Let us each day do, as mere exercises of discipline in moral gymnastics, a few acts that are disagreeable to us, the doing of which will help us in instant action in our hour of need. The exercises may be very simple: dropping for a time an intensely interesting book at the most thrilling page of the story; jumping out of bed at the first moment of waking; walking home when one is perfectly able to do so, but when the temptation is to take a car; talking to some disagreeable person and trying to make the conversation pleasant. These daily exercises in moral discipline will have a wondrous tonic effect on man's whole moral nature.

The individual can attain self-control in great things only through self-control in little things. He must study himself to discover what is the weak point in his armor, what is the element within him that ever keeps him from his fullest success. This is the characteristic upon which he should begin his exercise in self-control. Is it selfishness, vanity, cowardice, morbidness, temper, laziness, worry, mind-wandering, lack of purpose? Whatever form human weakness assumes in the masquerade of life he must discover. He must then live each day as if his whole existence were telescoped down to the single day before him. With no useless regret for the past, no useless worry for the future, he should live that day as if it were his only day, the only day left for him to assert all that is best in him, the only day left for him to conquer all that is worst in him. He should master the weak element within him at each slight manifestation from moment to moment. Each moment then must be a victory for it or for him. Will he be king or slave? The answer rests with him.

II

The Crimes of the Tongue

The second most deadly instrument of destruction is the gun—the first is the human tongue. The gun merely kills bodies; the tongue kills reputations and ofttimes ruins characters. Each gun works alone; each loaded tongue has a hundred accomplices. The havoc of the gun is visible at once, the full evil of the tongue lives through all the years. Even the eye of Omniscience might grow tired in tracing it to its finality.

The crimes of the tongue are words of unkindness, anger, malice, envy, bitterness, harsh criticism, gossip, lying and scandal. Theft and murder are awful crimes, yet in any single year the aggregate sorrow, pain and suffering they cause in a nation is microscopic when compared with the sorrows that come from the crimes of the tongue. Place in one of the scale-pans of justice the evils resulting from the acts of criminals, and in the other the grief and tears and suffering resulting from the crimes of respectability, and you will start back in amazement as you see the scale you thought the heavier shoot high in air.

At the hands of thief or murderer few of us suffer, even indirectly. But from the careless tongue of friend, the cruel tongue of enemy, who is free? No human being can live a life so true, so fair, so pure as to be beyond the reach of malice, or immune from the poisonous emanations of envy. The insidious attacks against one's reputation, the loathsome innuendoes, slurs, half-lies by which jealous mediocrity seeks to ruin its superiors, are like those insect parasites that kill the heart and life of a mighty oak. So cowardly is the method, so stealthy the shooting of the poisoned thorns, so insignificant the separate acts in their seeming, that one is not on guard against them. It is easier to dodge an elephant than a mircrobe.

Scandal is one of the crimes of the tongue, but it is only one. Every individual who breathes a word of scandal is an active stockholder in a society for the spread of moral contagion. He is instantly punished by Nature by having his mental eyes dimmed to sweetness and purity, and his mind deadened to the sunlight and glow of charity. There is developed a wondrous, ingenious perversion of mental vision by which every act of others is explained and interpreted from the lowest possible motives. They become like certain carrion flies that pass lightly over acres of rose-gardens to feast on a piece of putrid meat. They have developed a keen scent for the foul matter upon which they feed.

A man may lead a life of honesty and purity, battling bravely for all he holds dearest, so firm and sure of the rightness of his life that he never thinks for an instant of the diabolical ingenuity that makes evil and evil report where naught but good really exists. A few words lightly spoken by the tongue of slander, a significant expression of the eyes, a cruel shrug of the shoulders, with a pursing of the lips—and then friendly hands grow cold, the accustomed smile is displaced by a sneer, and one stands alone and aloof with a dazed feeling of wonder at the vague, intangible something that has caused it all.

For this craze for scandal, sensational newspapers of today are largely responsible. Each newspaper is not one tongue, but a thousand or a million tongues, telling the same foul story to as many

16

pairs of listening ears. The vultures of sensation-alism scent the carcass of immortality afar off. From the uttermost parts of the earth they collect the sin, disgrace and folly of humanity, and show them bare to the world. They do not even require *facts*, for morbid memories and fertile imaginations make even the worst of the world's happenings seem tame when compared with their monstrosities of invention. These stories, and the discussions they excite, develop in readers a cheap, shrewd power of distortion of the acts of all around them.

If a rich man gives a donation to some charity, they say: "He is doing it to get his name talked about, to help his business." If he gives it anonymously, they say, "Oh, it's some millionaire who is clever enough to know that refraining from giving his name will pique curiosity; he will see that the public is informed later." If he does not give to charity, they say: "Oh, he's stingy with his money, of course, like the rest of the millionaires." To the vile tongue of gossip, virtue is deemed a mask, noble ideals a pretense, generosity a bribe.

The man who stands above his fellows must expect to be the target for the envious arrows of their inferiority. It is part of the price he must pay for his advance. One of the most detestable characters in all literature is Iago. Envious of the promotion of Cassio above his head, he hated Othello. His was one of those low natures that become absorbed in sustaining his dignity, talking of "preserving his honor," forgetting it had so long been dead that even embalming could not preserve it. Day by day Iago dropped his poison; day by day did subtle resentment and studied vengeance distill the poison of distrust and suspicion into more powerfully insidious doses. With a mind wonderfully concentrated by the blackness of his purpose, he wove a network of circumstantial evidence around the pure-hearted Desdemona, and then murdered her vicariously, by the hand of Othello. Her very simplicity, confidence, innocence and artlessness made Desdemona the easier mark for the diabolic tactics of Iago.

Iago still lives in the hearts of thousands, who have all his despicable meanness without his cleverness. The constant dropping of their lying words of malice and envy have in too many instances worn away noble reputations of their superiors.

To sustain ourselves in our own hasty judgments we sometimes say, as we listen and accept without investigation the words of these modern Iagoes: "Well, where there is so much smoke, there must

18

be *some* fire." Yes, but the fire may be only the fire of malice, the incendiary firing of the reputation of another by the lighted torch of envy, thrown into the innocent facts of a life of superiority.

III

The Red Tape of Duty

Duty is the most over-lauded word in the whole vocabulary of life. Duty is the cold, bare anatomy of righteousness. Duty looks at life as a debt to be paid; love sees life as a debt to be collected. Duty is ever paying assessments; love is constantly counting its premiums.

Duty is forced, like a pump; love is spontaneous, like a fountain. Duty is prescribed and formal; it is part of the red tape of life. It means running on moral rails. It is good enough as a beginning; it is poor as a finality.

The boy who "stood on the burning deck," and who committed suicide on a technical point of obedience, has been held up to the school children of this century as a model of faithfulness to duty. The boy was the victim of a blind adherence to the red tape of duty. He was placing the whole responsibility for his acts on someone outside himself. He was helplessly waiting for instruction in the hour of emergency when he should have acted for himself. His act was an empty sacrifice. It was a useless throwing away of a human life.

The captain who goes down with his sinking vessel, when he has done everything in his power to save others and when he can save his own life without dishonor, is the victim of a false sense of duty. He is cruelly forgetful of the loved ones on shore that he is sacrificing. His death means a spectacular exit from life, the cowardly fear of an investigating committee, or a brave man's loyal, yet misguided, sense of duty. A human life with its wondrous possibilities, is too sacred an individual trust to be thus lightly thrown into eternity.

They tell us of the "sublime nobleness" of the Roman soldier at Pompeii, whose skeleton was found centuries afterward, imbedded in the once molten lava which swept down upon the doomed city. He was still standing at one of the gates, at his post of duty, still grasping a sword in his crumbling fingers. His was a morbid faithfulness to a discipline from which a great convulsion of Nature had released him. An automaton would have stood there just as boldly, just as uselessly.

The man who gives one hour of his life to loving, consecrated service to humanity is doing higher, better, truer work in the world than an army of Roman sentinels paying useless tribute to the red tape of duty. There is in this interpretation of duty no sympathy with the man who deserts his post when needed; it is but a protest against losing the essence, the reality of true duty in worshipping the mere form.

Duty is a hard, mechanical process for making men do things that love would make easy. It is a poor understudy to love. It is not a high enough motive with which to inspire humanity. Duty is the body to which love is the soul. Love, in the divine alchemy of life, transmutes all duties into privileges, all responsibilities into joys.

The workman who drops his tools at the stroke of twelve, as suddenly as if he had been struck by lightning, may be doing his duty, but he is doing nothing more. No man has made a great success of his life or a fit preparation for immortality by doing merely his duty. He must do that—and more. If love is in his work, the "more" will be easy.

The nurse may watch faithfully at the bedside of a sick child as a duty. But to the mother's heart the care of the little one, in the battle against death, is never a duty; the golden mantle of love thrown over every act makes the word "duty" have a jarring sound as if it were the voice of desecration.

When a child turns out badly in later years, the parent may say, "Well, I always did my duty by him." Then it is no wonder the boy turned out wrong. "Doing his duty by his son" too often implies merely food, lodging, clothes and education supplied by the father. Why, a public institution would give that! What the boy needed most was deep draughts of love; he needed to live in an atmosphere of sweet sympathy, counsel and trust. The parent should ever be an unfailing refuge, a constant resource and inspiration, not a mere larder, or hotel, or wardrobe, or school that furnishes these necessities free. The boast of parental duty is one of the dangers of modern society.

Christianity stands forth as the one religion based on love, not duty. Christianity sweeps all duties into one word—love. Love is the one great duty enjoined by the Christian religion. What duty creeps to laboriously, love reaches in a moment on the wings of a dove. Duty is not lost, condemned or destroyed in Christianity; it is dignified, purified and exalted and all its rough ways are made smooth by love.

23

The supreme instance of generosity in the world's history is not the giving of millions by someone of great name; it is the giving of a mite by a widow whose name does not appear. Behind the widow's mite was no sense of duty; it was the full, free and perfect gift of a heart filled with love. In the Bible "duty" is mentioned but five times; "love," hundreds.

In the conquest of any weakness in our mental or moral make-up, in the attainment of any strength, in our highest and truest relation to ourselves and to the world, let us ever make "love" our watchword, not mere "duty."

If we desire to live a life of truth and honesty, to make our word as strong as our bond, let us not expect to keep ourselves along the narrow line of truth under the constant lash of the whip of duty. Let us begin to love the truth, to fill our mind and life with the strong white light of sincerity and sterling honesty. Let us love the truth so strongly that there will develop within us, without our conscious effort, an ever-present horror of a lie.

If we desire to do good in the world, let us begin to love humanity, to realize more truly the great dominant note that sounds in every mortal, despite all the discords of life, the great natural bond of unity that makes all men brothers. Then jealousy, malice, envy, unkind words and cruel misjudging will be eclipsed and lost in love. Love is the wondrous angel of life that rolls away all the stones of sorrow and suffering from the pathway of duty.

IV

The Supreme Charity of the World

True charity is not typified by an alms-box. The benevolence of a checkbook does not meet all the wants of humanity. Giving food, clothing and money to the poor is only the beginning, the kindergarten class, of real charity. Charity has higher, purer forms of manifestation. Charity is but an instinctive reaching out for justice in life. Charity seeks to smooth down the rough places of living, to bridge the chasms of human sin and folly, to feed the heart-hungry, to give strength to the struggling, to be tender with human weakness, and greatest of all, it means obeying the Divine injunction: "Judge not."

The true symbol of the greatest charity is the scales of judgment held on high, suspended from the hand of justice. So perfectly are they poised that they are never at rest; they dare not stop for a moment to pronounce final judgment; each second adds its grain of evidence to either side of the balance. With this ideal before him, man, conscious of his own weakness and frailty, dare not arrogate to himself the Divine prerogative of pronouncing severe or final judgment on any individual. He will seek to train mind and heart to greater keenness, purity, and delicacy in watching the trembling movement of the balance in which he weighs the characters and reputations of those around him.

It is a great pity in life that all the greatest words are most degraded. We hear people say, "I do so love to study character, in the cars and on the street." They are not studying character; they are merely observing characteristics. The study of character is not a puzzle that a man may work out over night. Character is most subtle, elusive, changing and contradictory—a strange mingling of habits, hopes, tendencies, ideals, motives, weaknesses, traditions and memories—manifest in a thousand different phases.

There is but one quality necessary for the perfect understanding of character, one quality that, if man have it, he may *dare to judge*—that is, omniscience. Most people study character as a proof-reader pores over a great poem: his ears are dulled to the majesty and music of the lines, his eyes are darkened to the magic imagination of the genius of the author; that proofreader is busy watching for an inverted comma, a misspacing, or a wrong font letter. He has an eye trained for the imperfections, the weaknesses. Men who pride themselves on being shrewd in discovering the weak points, the vanity, dishonesty, immorality, intrigue and pettiness of others think they understand character. They know only part of character —they know only the depths to which some men may sink; they know not the heights to which some men may rise. An optimist is a man who has succeeded in associating with humanity for some time without becoming a cynic.

We never see the target a man aims at in life; we see only the target he hits. We judge from results, and we imagine an infinity of motives that we say must have been in his mind. No man since the creation has been able to live a life so pure and noble as to exempt him from the misjudgment of those around him.

If misfortune comes to someone, people are prone to say, "It is a judgment upon him." How do they know? Have they been eavesdropping at the door of Paradise? When sorrow and failure come to us, we regard them as misdirected packages that should be delivered elsewhere. We do too much watching of our neighbor's garden, too little weeding in our own.

Bottles have been picked up at sea thousands of miles from the point where they have been cast into the waters. They have been the sport of wind and weather; carried along by ocean currents, they have reached a destination undreamed of. Our flippant, careless words of judgment of the character of someone, words lightly and perhaps innocently spoken, may be carried by unknown currents and bring sorrow, misery and shame to the innocent. A cruel smile, a shrug of the shoulders or a cleverly eloquent silence may ruin in a moment the reputation a man or woman has been building for years. It is as a single motion of the hand may destroy the delicate geometry of a spider's web, spun from its own body and life, though any human effort could not restore it.

We do not need to judge nearly so much as we think we do. This is the age of snap judgments. The habit is greatly intensified by the sensational press. Twenty-four hours after a great murder there is difficulty in getting enough men who have not already formulated a judgment, to try the case. These men, in most instances, have read and accepted the garbled, highly-colored newspaper account; they have to their own satisfaction discovered the murderer, practically tried him and sentenced him. We hear readers state their decisions with all the force and absoluteness of one who has had the whole Book of Life made luminant and spread out before him. If there be one place in life where the attitude of the agnostic is beautiful, it is in this matter of judging others. It is the courage to say, "I don't know. I am waiting further evidence. I must hear both sides of the question." It is this suspended judgment that is the supreme form of charity.

It is strange that in life we recognize the right of every criminal to have a fair, open trial, yet we condemn unheard the dear friends around us on mere circumstantial evidence. We rely on the mere evidence of our senses, trust it implicitly, and permit it to sweep away like a mighty tide the faith that has been ours for years. We see all life grow dark, hope sink before our eyes, and the golden treasures of memory turn to cruel thoughts of loss to sting us with maddening pain. If we be thus unjust to those we hold dear, what must be the cruel injustice of our judgment of others?

We know nothing of the trials, sorrows and temptations of those around us, of pillows wet with sobs, of the life-tragedy that may be hidden behind a smile, of the secret cares, struggles and worries that shorten life and leave their mark in hair prematurely whitened, and in character changed and almost re-created in a few days.

Let us not dare to add to the burden of another the pain of our judgment. If we would guard our lips from expressing, we must control our mind, we must stop this continual sitting in judgment on the acts of others, even in private. Let us by daily exercises in self-control learn to turn off the process of judging—as we would turn off the gas. Let us eliminate pride, passion, personal feeling, prejudice and pettiness from our mind, and higher, purer emotions will rush in, as air seeks to fill a vacuum. Charity is not a formula; it is an atmosphere. Let us cultivate charity in judging; let us seek to draw out latent good in others rather than to discover hidden evil. It requires the eye of charity to see the undeveloped butterfly in the caterpillar. Let us, if we would rise to the full glory of our privilege, to the dignity of true living, make for our watchword the injunction of the supreme charity of the world—"Judge not."

V

Worry, the Great American Disease

Worry is the most popular form of suicide. Worry
impairs appetite, disturbs sleep, makes respira-
tion irregular, spoils digestion, irritates disposition, warps character, weakens mind, stimulates
disease, and saps bodily health. It is the real
cause of death in thousands of instances where
some other disease is named in the death certifi-
cate. Worry is mental poison; work is mental food.

When a man or woman works over in dreams
the problems of the day, when the sleeping hours
are spent in turning the kaleidoscope of the day's
activities, then there is either overwork or worry,
and most likely it is the worry that comes from
overwork. The Creator never intended a healthy
mind to dream of the day's duties. Either dream-
less sleep or dreams of the past should be the order
of the night.

When the spectre of one grief, one fear, one sorrow, obtrudes itself between the eye and the printed page; when the inner voice of this irritating memory, or fear, looms up so loud as to deaden outside voices, there is danger to the individual. When all day, every hour, every moment, there is the dull, insistent, numb pain of something that makes itself felt through, above and below all our other thinking, we must know that we are worrying. Then there is but one thing to do—we must stop that worry; we must kill it.

Worry is forethought gone to seed. Worry is discounting possible future sorrows so that the individual may have present misery. Worry is the father of insomnia. Worry is the traitor in our camp that dampens our powder, weakens our aim. Under the guise of helping us to bear the present, and to be ready for the future, worry multiplies enemies within our own mind to sap our strength.

Worry is the dominance of the mind by a single vague, restless, unsatisfied, fearing and fearful idea. The mental energy and force that should be concentrated on the successive duties of the day is constantly and surreptitiously abstracted and absorbed by this one fixed idea. The full rich strength of the *unconscious* working of the mind,

33

that which produces our best success, that represents our finest activity, is tapped, led away and wasted on worry.

Worry must not be confused with anxiety, though both words agree in meaning, originally, a "choking," or a "strangling," referring, of course, to the throttling effect upon individual activity. Anxiety faces large issues of life seriously, calmly, with dignity. Anxiety always suggests hopeful possibility; it is active in being ready, and devising measures to meet the outcome. Worry is not one large individual sorrow; it is a colony of petty, vague, insignificant, restless imps of fear, that become important only from their combination, their constancy, their iteration.

When death comes, when the one we love has passed from us, and the silence and the loneness and the emptiness of all things make us stare dry-eyed into the future, we give ourselves up, for a time, to the agony of isolation. This is not a petty worry we must kill ere it kills us. This is the awful majesty of sorrow that mercifully benumbs us, though it may later become, in the mysterious working of omnipotence, a rebaptism and a regeneration. It is the worry *habit*, the constant magnifying of petty sorrows to eclipse the sun of happiness, against which I here make protest.

To cure worry, the individual must be his own physician; he must give the case heroic treatment. He must realize, with every fibre of his being, the utter, absolute uselessness of worry. He must not think this is commonplace, a bit of mere theory; it is a reality that he must translate for himself from mere words to a real, living fact. He must fully understand that if it were possible for him to spend a whole series of eternities in worry, it would not change the fact one jot or tittle. It is a time for action, not worry, because worry paralyzes thought and action, too. If you set down a column of figures in addition, no amount of worry can change the sum total of those figures. That result is wrapped up in the inevitability of mathematics. The result can be made different only by changing the figures as they are set down, one by one, in that column.

The one time that a man cannot afford to worry is when he *does* worry. Then he is facing, or imagines he is, a critical turn in affairs. This is the time when he needs one hundred per cent of his mental energy to make his plans quickly, to see what is his wisest decision, to keep a clear eye on

the sky and on his course, and a firm hand on the
helm until he has weathered the storm in safety.

There are two reasons why man should not
worry, either one of which must operate in every
instance. First, because he *cannot* prevent the results he fears. Second, because he *can* prevent
them. If he be powerless to avert the blow, he
needs perfect mental concentration to meet it
bravely, to lighten its force, to get what salvage he
can from the wreck, to sustain his strength at this
time when he must plan a new future. If he *can*
prevent the evil he fears, then he has no need to
worry, for he would by so doing be dissipating
energy in his very hour of need.

If man does, day by day, ever the best he can by
the light he has, he has no need to fear, no need
to regret, no need to worry. No agony of worry
would do aught to help him. Neither mortal nor
angel can do more than his best. If we look back
upon our past life we will see how, in the marvelous working of events, the cities of our greatest
happiness and of our fullest success have been built
along the rivers of our deepest sorrows, our most
abject failures. We then realize that our present
happiness or success would have been impossible
had it not been for some terrible affliction or loss

in the past, some wondrous potent force in the evolution of our character or our fortune.

To cure one's self of worry is not an easy task; it is not to be removed in two or three applications of the quack medicine of any cheap philosophy, but it requires only clear, simple, common sense applied to the business of life. Man has no right to waste his own energies, to weaken his own powers and influence, for he has inalienable duties to himself, to his family, to society, and to the world.

VI

The Greatness of Simplicity

Simplicity is the elimination of the nonessential in all things. It reduces life to its minimum of real needs; raises it to its maximum of powers. Simplicity means the survival, not of the fittest, but of the best. In morals it kills the weeds of vice and weakness so that the flowers of virtue and strength may have room to grow. Simplicity cuts off waste and intensifies concentration. It converts flickering torches into searchlights.

All great truths are simple. The essence of Christianity could be given in a few words; a lifetime would be but continued seeking to make those words real and living in thoughts and acts. The true Christian's individual belief is always simpler than his church creed, and upon these vital, foundation elements he builds his life. Higher criticism never rises to the heights of his simplicity. He does not care whether the whale swallowed Jonah or Jonah swallowed the whale. Hairsplitting interpretation of words and phrases is an intellectual dissipation he has no time for. He cares naught for the anatomy of religion; he has its soul. His simple faith he lives in thought and word and act, day by day. Like the lark he lives nearest the ground; like the lark he soars highest toward heaven.

The minister whose sermons are made up merely of flowers of rhetoric, sprigs of quotation, sweet fancy, and perfumed commonplaces, is—consciously or unconsciously—posing in the pulpit. His literary charlotte-russes, sweet froth on a spongy, pulpy base, never helped a human soul; they give neither strength nor inspiration. If the mind and heart of the preacher were really thrilled with the greatness and simplicity of religion, he would, week by week, apply the ringing truths of his faith to the vital problems of daily living. The test of a strong, simple sermon is results—not the Sunday praise of his auditors, but their bettered lives during the week. People who pray on their knees on Sunday and prey on their neighbors on Monday need simplicity in their faith.

No character can be simple unless it is based on

truth, unless it is lived in harmony with one's own conscience and ideals. Simplicity is the pure white light of a life lived from within. It is destroyed by any attempt to live in harmony with public opinion. Public opinion is a conscience owned by a syndicate, where the individual is merely a stockholder. But the individual has a conscience of which he is sole proprietor. Adjusting his life to his own ideals is the royal road to simplicity. Affectation is the confession of inferiority; it is an unnecessary proclamation that one is not living the life he pretends to live.

Simplicity is restful contempt for the nonessentials of life. It is restless hunger for the nonessentials that is the secret of most of the discontent of the world. It is constant striving to outshine others that kills simplicity and happiness.

Nature, in all her revelations, seeks to teach man he greatness of simplicity. Health is but the iving of a physical life in harmony with a few simple, clearly defined laws. Simple food, simple exercise, simple precautions will work wonders. But man grows tired of the simple things, he yields to subtle temptations in eating and drinking, listens to his palate instead of to Nature—and he suffers. He is then led into intimate acquaintance with

40

dyspepsia, and he sits like a child at his own boun-
teous table, forced to limit his eating to simple
food that he scorned.

There is a tonic strength in the hour of sorrow
and affliction, in escaping from the world and society and getting back to the simple duties and in-
terests we have slighted and forgotten. Our world
grows smaller, but it grows dearer and greater.
Simple things have a new charm for us, and we
suddenly realize that we have been renouncing all
that is best in our pursuit of some phantom.

Simplicity is the characteristic that is most difficult to simulate. The signature that is most difficult to imitate is the one that is most simple, most
individual and most free from flourishes. The
bank note that is the most difficult to counterfeit
successfully is the one that contains the fewest lines
and has the least intricate detail. So simple is it that
any departure from the normal is instantly ap-
parent. So is it also in mind and in morals.

Simplicity in act is the outward expression of
simplicity in thought. Men who carry on their
shoulders the fate of a nation are quiet, modest,
unassuming. They are often made gentle, calm and
simple by the discipline of their responsibility.
They have no room in their minds for the pettiness

of personal vanity. It is ever the drum major who grows pompous when he thinks that the whole world is watching him as he marches at the head of the procession. The great general, bowed with the honors of many campaigns, is simple and unaffected as a child.

The longest Latin derivatives seem necessary to express the thoughts of young writers. The world's great masters in literature can move mankind to tears, give light and life to thousands in darkness and doubt, or scourge a nation for its folly, by words so simple as to be commonplace. But transfigured by the divinity of genius, there seems almost a miracle in words.

Life grows wondrously beautiful when we look at it as simple, when we can brush aside the trivial cares and sorrows and worries and failures and say, "They don't count. They are not the real things of life; they are but interruptions. There is something within me, my individuality, that makes all these gnats of trouble seem too trifling for me to permit them to have any dominion over me." Simplicity is a mental soil where artifice, lying, and selfish, low ambition cannot grow.

The man whose character is simple looks truth and honesty so straight in the face that he has no consciousness of intrigue and corruption around him. He is deaf to the hints and whispers of wrong that a suspicious nature would suspect even before they existed. He scorns to meet intrigue with intrigue, to hold power by bribery, to pay weak tribute to an inferior who has a temporary inning. To true simplicity, to perceive a truth is to begin to live it, to see a duty is to begin to do it. Nothing great can ever enter into the consciousness of a man of simplicity and remain but a theory. Simplicity in a character is like the needle of a compass—it knows only one point, its North, its ideal.

Let us seek to cultivate this simplicity in all things in our life. The first step toward simplicity is "simplifying." The beginning of mental or moral progress or reform is always renunciation or sacrifice. It is rejection, surrender or destruction of separate phrases of habit or life that have kept us from higher things. Reform your diet and you simplify it; make your speech truer and higher and you simplify it; reform your morals and you begin to cut off your immorals. The secret of all true greatness is simplicity. Make simplicity the keynote of your life and you will be great, no matter though your life be humble and your influence seem but little.

Simplicity is never to be associated with weakness and ignorance. It means reducing tons of ore to nuggets of gold. It means the light of fullest knowledge; it means that the individual has seen the folly and the nothingness of those things that make up the sum of the life of others. He has lived *down* what others are blindly seeking to live *up* to. Simplicity is the sun of a self-centered and pure life—the secret of any specific greatness in the life of the individual.

VII

Living Life over Again

During a terrific storm a ship was driven far out
of her course, and, helpless and disabled, was carried into a strange bay. The water supply gave
out, and the crew suffered agony of thirst, yet
dared not drink of the salt water in which their
vessel floated. In their last extremity they lowered
a bucket over the ship's side, and in desperation
quaffed the beverage they thought was sea water.
But to their joy and amazement the water was
fresh, cool and life-giving. They were in a fresh-
water arm of the sea, and they did not know it.
They had simply to reach down and accept the
new life and strength for which they prayed.

Man, today heart-weary with the sorrow, sin and
failure of his past life, feels that he could live a
better life if he could only have another chance, if
he could only live life over again, if he could only

start afresh with his present knowledge and experience. He looks back with regretful memory to the golden days of youth and sadly mourns his wasted chances. He then turns hopefully to the thought of a life to come. But, helpless, he stands between the two ends of life, yet thirsting for the chance to live a new life, according to his bettered condition for living it. In his blindness and unknowing, he does not realize, like the storm-driven sailors, that the new life is all around him; he has but to reach out and take it. Every day is a new life, every sunrise but a new birth for himself and the world, every morning the beginning of a new existence for him, a new, great chance to put to new uses the results of his past living.

The man who looks back upon his past life and says, "I have nothing to regret," has lived in vain. The life without regret is the life without gain. Regret is but the light of fuller wisdom from our past, illumining our future. It means that we are wiser today than we were yesterday. This new wisdom means new responsibility, new privileges; it is a new chance for a better life. But if regret remains merely "regret," it is useless; it must become the revelation of new possibilities, and the inspiration and source of strength to realize them.

Even omnipotence could not change the past, but each man, to a degree far beyond his knowing, holds his future in his own hands.

If man were sincere in his longing to live life over he would get more help from his failures. If he realizes his wasted golden hours of opportunity, let him not waste other hours in useless regret, but seek to forget his folly and to keep before him only the lessons of it. His past extravagance of time should lead him to minimize his loss by marvelous economy of present moments. If his whole life be darkened by the memory of a cruel wrong he has done another, if direct amends be impossible to the injured one who has passed from life, let him make the world the legatee to receive his expressions of restitution. Let his regret and sorrow be manifest in words of kindness and sympathy, and acts of sweetness and love given to all with whom he comes in contact. If he regrets a war he has made against one individual, let him place the entire world on his pension list. If a man makes a certain mistake once, the only way he can properly express his recognition of it is not to make a similar mistake later.

There are many people in this world who want to live life over because they take such pride in their past. They resemble the beggars in the street who tell you they "have seen better days." It is not what man *was* that shows character; it is what he progressively *is*. Trying to obtain a present record on a dead past is like some present-day mediocrity that tries to live on its ancestry. We look for the fruit in the branches of the family tree, not in the roots. Showing how a family degenerated from a noble ancestor of generations ago to its present representative is not a boast—it is an unnecessary confession. Let man think less of his own ancestors and more of those he is preparing for his posterity; less of his past virtue, and more of his future.

When man pleads for a chance to live life over, there is always an implied plea of inexperience, of a lack of knowledge. This is unworthy even of a coward. We know the laws of health, yet we ignore them or defy them every day. We know what is the proper food for us to eat, yet we gratify our appetites and trust to our cleverness to square the account with Nature somehow. We know that success is a matter of simple, clearly defined laws, of the development of mental essentials, of tireless energy and concentration, of constant payment of price—we know all this, and yet we do not live up to our knowledge. We constantly eclipse ourselves by ourselves, and then we blame Fate.

Man's only plea for a chance to live life again is that he has gained in wisdom and experience. If he is really in earnest, then he can live life over, he can live life anew, he can live the new life that comes to him day by day. Let him leave to the past, to the aggregated thousands of yesterdays, all their mistakes, sin, sorrow, misery and folly, and start afresh. Let him close the books of his old life, let him strike a balance and start anew, crediting himself with all the wisdom he has gained from his past failure and weakness, and charging himself with the new duties and responsibilities that come from the possession of his new capital of wisdom. Let him criticize others less and himself more, and start out bravely in this new life he is to live.

What the world needs is more day-to-day living; starting in the morning with fresh, clear ideals for that day, and seeking to live that day, and each successive hour and moment of that day, as if it were all time and all eternity. This has in it no element of disregard for the future, for each day is set in harmony with that future. It is like the sea captain heading his vessel toward his port of destination, and day by day keeping her steaming toward it. This view of living kills morbid regret of the past and morbid worry about the future. Most people want large, guaranteed slices of life; they would not be satisfied with manna fresh every day, as was given to the children of Israel; they want grain elevators filled with daily bread.

Life is worth living if it is lived in a way that is worth living. Man does not own his life to do with as he will. He has merely a life-interest in it. He must finally surrender it—with an accounting. At each New Year it is common to make new resolutions, but in the true life of the individual each day is the beginning of a New Year if he will only make it so. A mere date on the calendar of eternity is no more a divider of time than a particular grain of sand divides the desert.

Let us not make heroic resolutions so far beyond our strength that the resolution becomes a dead memory within a week; but let us promise ourselves that each day will be the new beginning of a newer, better and truer life for ourselves, for those around us, and for the world.

VIII

Syndicating Our Sorrows

The most selfish man in the world is the one who is most unselfish with his sorrows. He does not leave a single misery of his untold to you, or unsuffered by you—he gives you all of them. The world becomes to him a syndicate formed to take stock in his private cares, worries and trials. His mistake is in forming a syndicate; he should organize a trust and control it all himself, then he could keep his misery to himself.

Life is a great, serious problem for the individual. All our greatest joys and our deepest sorrows come to us—alone. We must go into our Gethsemane—alone. We must battle against the mighty weakness within us—alone. We must live our own life—alone. We must die—alone. We must accept the full responsibility of our life—alone. If each

51

one of us has this mighty problem of life to solve for himself, if each of us has his own cares, responsibilities, failures, doubts, fears, bereavements, we surely are playing a coward's part when we syndicate our sorrows to others.

We should seek to make life brighter for others; we should seek to hearten them in their trials by the example of our courage in bearing our sorrows. We should seek to forget our failures, and remember only the new wisdom they gave us; we should live down our griefs by counting the joys and privileges still left to us; put behind us our worries and regrets, and face each new day of life as bravely as we can. But we have no right to retail our sorrow through the community.

Autobiography constitutes a large part of the conversation of some people. It is not really conversation; it is an uninterrupted monologue. These people study their individual lives with a microscope, and then they throw an enlarged view of their miseries on a screen and lecture on them, as a scientist discourses on the microbes in a drop of water. They tell you that "they did not sleep a wink all night; they heard the clock strike every quarter of an hour." Now, there is no real cause for thus boasting of insomnia. It requires no peculiar talent, even though it does come only to wide-awake people.

If you ask such a man how he is feeling, he will trace the whole genealogy of his present condition down from the time he had the grippe four years ago. You hoped for a word; he gives you a treatise. You asked for a sentence; he delivers an encyclopedia. His motto is, "Every man his own Boswell." He is syndicating his sorrows.

The woman who makes her trials with her children, her troubles with her servants, her difficulties with her family, the subjects of conversation with her callers is syndicating her sorrows.

The business man who lets his dyspepsia get into his disposition, and who makes everyone around him suffer because he himself is ill, is syndicating ill health. We have no right to make others the victims of our moods. If illness makes us cross and irritable, makes us unjust to faithful workers who cannot protest, let us quarantine ourselves so that we do not spread the contagion. Let us force ourselves to speak slowly, to keep anger away from the eyes, to prevent temper showing in the voice. If we feel that we *must* have dyspepsia, let us keep it out of our head; let us keep it from getting north of the neck.

Most people sympathize too much with themselves. They take themselves as a single sentence isolated from the great text of life. They study themselves too much as separated from the rest of humanity, instead of being vitally connected with their fellow men. There are some people who surrender to sorrow as others give way to dissipation. There is a vain pride of sorrow as well as of beauty. Most individuals have a strange glow of vanity in looking back upon their past and feeling that few others in life have suffered such trials, hardships and disappointments as they have.

When death comes into the little circle of loved ones who make up our world, all life becomes dark to us. We seem to have no reason for existing, no object, no incentive, no hope. The love that made struggle and effort bearable for us is gone. We stare, dry-eyed, into the future, and see no future; we want none. Life has become to us a past with no future, a memory without hope.

Then in the divine mystery of Nature's processes, under the tender, soothing touch of Time, as days melt into weeks, we begin to open our eyes gently to the world around us, and the noise and tumult of life jars less and less upon us. We have become emotionally convalescent. As the days go on, in our deep love, in the fullness of our loyalty, we protest often, with tears in our eyes, against our gradual return to the spirit and atmosphere of the days of the past. We feel in a subtle way a new pain, as if we were disloyal to the dear one, as if we were faithless to our love. Nature sweetly turns aside our protesting hands, and says to us, "There is no disloyalty in permitting the wounds to lessen their pain, to heal gradually, if Time foreordains that they can heal." There are some natures, all-absorbed in a mighty love, wherein no healing is possible, but these are rare souls in life.

Bitter though our anguish be, we have no right to syndicate our sorrow. We have no right to cast a gloom over happy natures by our heavy weight of crepe, by serving the term prescribed by society for wearing the livery of mourning—as if real grief thought of a uniform. We have no right to syndicate our grief by using note paper with a heavy black border as wide as a hatband, thus parading our personal sorrow to others in their happiest moments.

If life has not gone well with us, if fortune has left us disconsolate, if love has grown cold, and we sit alone by the embers; if life has become to us a valley of desolation, through which weary limbs must drag an unwilling body till the end shall come, let us not radiate such an atmosphere to those around us; let us not take strangers through the catacombs of our life, and show the bones of our dead past; let us not pass our cup of sorrow to others, but, if we must drink it, let us take it as Socrates did his poison hemlock— grandly, heroically and uncomplainingly.

If your life has led you to doubt the existence of honor in man and virtue in woman; if you feel that religion is a pretense, that spirituality is a sham, that life is a failure, and death the entrance to nothingness; if you have absorbed all the poison philosophy of the world's pessimists, and committed the folly of believing it, don't syndicate it.

If your fellow man is clinging to one frail spar, the last remnant of a noble, shipwrecked faith in God and humanity, let him keep it. Do not loosen his fingers from his hope, and tell him it is a delusion. How do you know? Who told you it was so?

If these high-tide moments of life sweep your faith in Omnipotence into nothingness, if the friend in whom you have put all faith in humanity and humanity's God betrays you, do not eagerly accept the teachings of those modern freethinkers who syndicate their infidelity at so much per reserved seat. Seek to recover your lost faith by listening to the million voices that speak of infinite wisdom, infinite love, that manifest themselves in nature and humanity, and then build up as rapidly as you can a new faith, a faith in something higher, better and truer than you have known before.

You may have *one* in the world to whom you may dare show with the fullness of absolute confidence and perfect faith any thought, any hope, any sorrow, but you dare not trust them to the world. Do not show the world through your Bluebeard chamber; keep your trials and sorrows as close to you as you can till you have mastered them. Don't weaken others by syndicating miseries.

IX

The Revelations of Reserve Power

Every individual is a marvel of unknown and un-realized possibilities. Nine-tenths of an iceberg is always below water. Nine-tenths of the possibilities of good and evil of the individual is ever hidden from his sight.

Burns' prayer that we might "see ourselves as others see us," was weak. The answer could minister only to man's vanity; it would show him only what others think him to be, not what he is. We should pray to see ourselves as we *are*. But no man could face the radiant revelation of the latent powers and forces within him, underlying the weak, narrow life he is living. He would fall blinded and prostrate as did Moses before the burning bush. Man is not a mechanical music-box wound up by the Creator and set to play a fixed number of prescribed tunes. He is a human harp, with infinite possibilities of unawakened music.

The untold revelations of Nature are in her reserve power. Reserve power is Nature's method of meeting emergencies. Nature is wise and economic. Nature saves energy and effort, and gives only what is absolutely necessary for life and development under any given condition, and when new needs arise, Nature always meets them by her reserve power.

In animal life Nature reveals this in a million phases. Animals placed in the darkness of the Mammoth Cave gradually have the sense of sight weakened and the senses of smell, touch and hearing intensified. Nature watches over all animals, making their color harmonize with the general tone of their surroundings to protect them from their enemies. Those arctic animals which in the summer inhabit regions free from snow, turn white when winter comes. In the desert, the lion, the camel and all the desert antelopes have more or less the color of the sand and rocks among which they live. In tropical forests parrots are usually green; turacous, barbets and bee-eaters have a preponderance of green in their plumage. The colors change as the habits of the animals change from generation to generation. Nature, by her reserve power, always meets the new needs of animals with new strength, new harmony with new conditions.

About a century ago three pairs of enterprising rabbits were introduced into Australia. Today, the increase of these six immigrants may be counted by millions. They became a pest to the country. Fortunes have been spent to exterminate them. Wire fences many feet high and thousands of miles long have been built to keep out the invaders. The rabbits had to fight awful odds to live, but they have now outwitted man. They have developed a new nail, a long nail by which they can retain their hold on the fence while climbing. With this same nail they can burrow six or eight inches under the netting, and thus enter the fields that mean food and life to them. They are now laughing at man. Reserve power has vitalized for these rabbits latent possibilities because they did not tamely accept their condition, but in their struggle to live learned *how* to live.

In plant life, Nature is constantly revealing reserve power. The possibilities of almost infinite color are present in every green plant, even in roots and stems. Proper conditions only are needed to reveal them. By obeying Nature's laws, man could make leaves as beautifully colored as flowers. The wild rose has only a single corolla; but, when cultivated in rich soil, the numerous yellow stamens change into the brilliant red leaves of the full-grown cabbage-rose. This is but one of Nature's miracles of reserve power. Once the banana was a tropical lily, the peach was at one time a bitter almond. To tell the full story of reserve power in Nature would mean to write the history of the universe, in a thousand volumes.

Nature is a great believer in "double engines." Man is equipped with nearly every organ in duplicate—eyes, ears, lungs, arms and legs, so that if one be weakened, its mate, through reserve power, is stimulated to do enough for both. Even where the organ itself is not duplicated, as in the nose, there is a division of parts so there is constant reserve. Nature, for still further protection, has for every part of the body an understudy in training, to be ready in a crisis, as the sense of touch for the blind.

Birds, when frightened, ruffle their feathers; a dog that has been in the water shakes its coat so that each hair stands out of itself; the startled hedgehog projects every quill. These actions are produced by "skin muscles" that are rudimentary in man, and over which, in ordinary conditions, he has no control. But in a moment of terrible fear, reserve power quickens their action in a second, and the hair on his head "stands on end" in the intensity of his fright.

Nature, that thus watches so tenderly over the physical needs of man, is equally provident in storing for him a mental and a moral reserve power. Man may fail in a dozen different lines of activity and then succeed brilliantly in a phase wherein he was unconscious of any ability. We must never rest content with what we *are*, and say, "There is no use for me to try. I can never be great. I am not even clever now." But the law of reserve power stands by us as a fairy godmother and says, "There is one charm by which you can transmute the dull dross of your present condition into the pure gold of strength and power—that charm is ever doing your best, ever daring more. The full measure of your final attainment can never be told in advance. Rely upon me to help you with new revelations of strength in new emergencies. Never be cast down because your power seems so trifling, your progress so slow. The world's greatest and best men were failures in some line, failures many times before failure was crowned with success."

There is in the mythology of the Norsemen a belief that the strength of an enemy we kill enters into us. This is true in character. As we conquer a passion, a thought, a feeling, a desire; as we rise superior to some impulse, the strength of that victory, trifling though it may be, is stored by Nature as a reserve power for us in the hour of our need.

Were we to place before almost any individual the full chart of his future—his trials, sorrows, failures, afflictions, loss, sickness and loneliness—and ask him if he could bear it, he would say, "No! I could not bear all that and live." But he *can* and he *does*. The hopes upon the realization of which he has staked all his future turn to air as he nears them; friends whom he has trusted betray him; the world grows cold to him; the child whose smile is the light of his life dishonors his name; death takes from him the wife of his heart. Reserve power has been watching over him and ever giving him new strength, even while he sleeps.

If we are conscious of any weakness, and desire to conquer it, we can force ourselves into positions where we *must* act in a way to strengthen ourselves through that weakness, cut off our retreat, burn our bridges behind us, and fight like Spartans till the victory is ours.

Reserve power is like the manna given to the children of Israel in the wilderness; only enough was given them to keep them for one day. Each successive day had its new supply of strength. There is in the leaning tower of Pisa a spiral stairway so steep in its ascent that only one step at a time is revealed to us. But as each step is taken the next is made visible, and thus, step by step, to the very highest. So in the Divine economy of the universe, reserve power is a gradual and constant revelation of strength within us to meet each new need. And no matter what our line of life, what our need, we should feel that we have within us infinite, untried strength and possibility, and that, if we believe and do our best, the Angel of reserve power will walk by our side, and will even divide the waters of the Red Sea of our sorrows and trials so we may walk through in safety.